MATTHEW HOLLETT

ALBUM ROCK

Looking back through the lens of Paul-Émile Miot

BOULDER
PUBLICATIONS

Library and Archives Canada Cataloguing in Publication

Hollett, Matthew, 1982-, author
    Album rock : looking back through the lens of Paul-Émile Miot
/ Matthew Hollett.

ISBN 978-1-77523-455-5 (softcover)

    1. Miot, Paul-Émile, 1827-1900--Poetry. I. Title.

PS8615.O4373A79 2018   C818'.607   C2018-903966-3
© 2018 Matthew Hollett

Design and layout: Todd Manning
Editor: Stephanie Porter
Copy editor: Iona Bulgin
Printed in Canada

We acknowledge the financial support of the Government of Newfoundland and Labrador through the Department of Tourism, Culture and Recreation.

Newfoundland Labrador

Funded by the Government of Canada   Financé par le gouvernement du Canada

TABLE OF CONTENTS

Rocher peint par les marins français (Rock painted by French sailors), Paul-Émile Miot.

Paul-Émile Miot and photography were born in the same heartbeat of history. Miot was born in 1827, and the earliest known surviving photograph was made by Niépce in 1826 or 1827. Though Miot would spend most of his life in the French navy, he was born in Trinidad. His grandfather, a French merchant, had crossed the Atlantic in search of opportunity, and Miot would follow suit, crossing ocean after ocean in his long career as a naval officer. Fascinated by the new science called *photography,* he would bring his camera to places where cameras had never been.

Miot made the photograph titled *Rocher peint par les marins français (Rock painted by French sailors)* between 1857 and 1859, during one of his first voyages to Newfoundland. It's a curious, almost cartoonish scene. French sailors pose with paintbrushes and a ladder, having painted the word *Album* on a large rock in Ship Cove, Sacred Bay, on the Great Northern Peninsula. The peculiar word resounds over the water, as if the rock is calling out its name. One hundred and sixty-odd years later, though the paint is long gone, the landmark is still known as Album Rock.

The man standing atop the rock is not Paul-Émile Miot. Still, if I look for the photographer's presence in the photo, I find it in this figure. Contemplative, poised, surveying the coastline. Anchored to the earth but adrift against a vacant sky, as Miot must have stood so many times on the deck of a ship, steadying his camera. Reckoning distances, the lay of the landscape, the play of light on water.

St. John's is like a black and white photograph on the morning we leave to drive across the island. The horizon and the highway are the same mottled grey. It's early July, and summer is slowly breaking through the concrete cloud banks of the Avalon.

By the time we reach Clarenville, though, a blue sky promises to hitch a ride all the way to Gros Morne. My friend Rosie and I will camp in the park before continuing up the Northern Peninsula tomorrow. We're travelling across a big rock in search of a smaller one.

Only the dotted yellow stitches of the median seem to keep the patchwork asphalt from falling apart. The roadside is a dark swath of spruce peppered with purple lupins. Every rocky outcrop is a page from an address book, full of names graffitied in white paint. *Jessie ❤'s Kevin. Davy + Nancy.* On a gravelly hillside near Terra Nova, people have painstakingly placed white stones to spell out larger declarations.

We reach Gros Morne in the early evening. Rosie slows the car, glancing out at the shale embankments along the side of the road, and says she wants to show me something. She pulls over. There's dust in the air from the car tires, and when we wade into the brush, dust clings to our legs. Rosie wanders along the wayside and soon spots what she's looking for: a heavy slab of stone laid upright against the slope. She tips it aside to reveal a pattern of indentations like rippling waves.

It takes me a moment to see the trilobite, as large as a dinner plate. Rosie tells me her father first showed her the fossil 20 years before. There are no signs or interpretive panels, but locals know about it. Rosie likes to visit it when she drives by. I take a few photos, wishing I could swivel the sun so that its light would better bring out the picture etched into the stone.

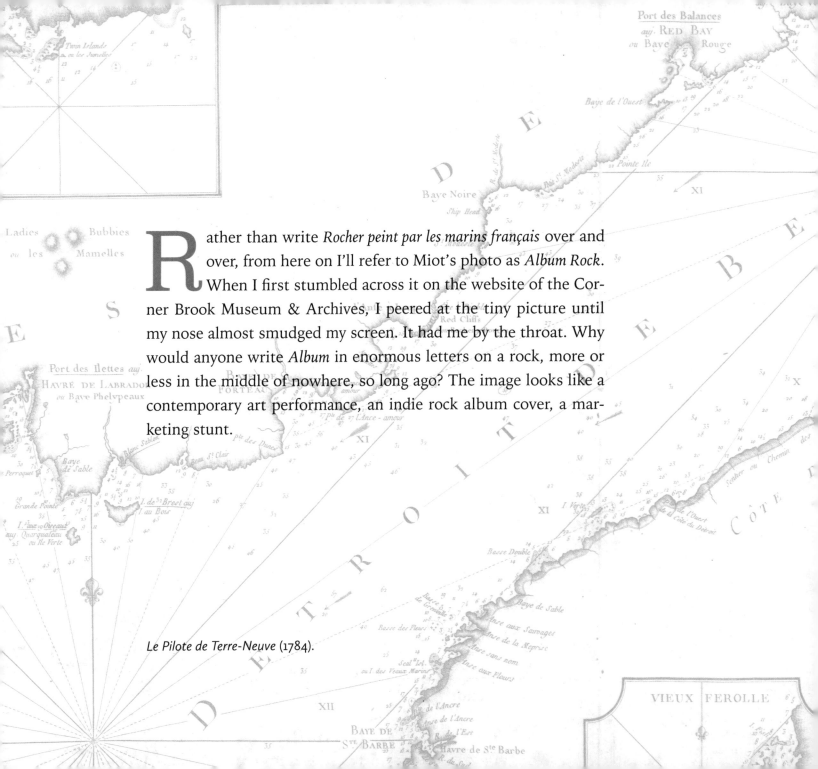

Rather than write *Rocher peint par les marins français* over and over, from here on I'll refer to Miot's photo as *Album Rock*. When I first stumbled across it on the website of the Corner Brook Museum & Archives, I peered at the tiny picture until my nose almost smudged my screen. It had me by the throat. Why would anyone write *Album* in enormous letters on a rock, more or less in the middle of nowhere, so long ago? The image looks like a contemporary art performance, an indie rock album cover, a marketing stunt.

Le Pilote de Terre-Neuve (1784).

At the same time, I'm charmed by the photograph's implausible dignity. Atop a wind-blasted crag, a sailor poses, aloof, as if in deep thought. There is yearning in the stylized detail of the lettering, every serif carefully in place despite being bedraggled by the rocky surface. The picture is scuffed and scratched, seemingly as timeworn as the boulder it depicts.

When I look up Ship Cove on a map, the notched peninsula is itself like a serif on the glyph of Newfoundland. The photograph is full of visual echoes that resonate with me. It bounced around my hard drive and my mind for four years before I finally wrote a small grant proposal to research it, including a field trip to Sacred Bay.

On the day I submitted my proposal, the top national news headline was the collapse of one of New Brunswick's famous Hopewell Rocks. After tens of thousands of years, Elephant Rock had finally given in to the gentle nudging of the tide, 200 tonnes of stone crashing into the seabed overnight. I wondered how much Album Rock might have changed, and how hard it would be to locate. If I travelled 1,065 kilometres from St. John's to Ship Cove, what would I find?

Chart of the island of Newfoundland (1801).

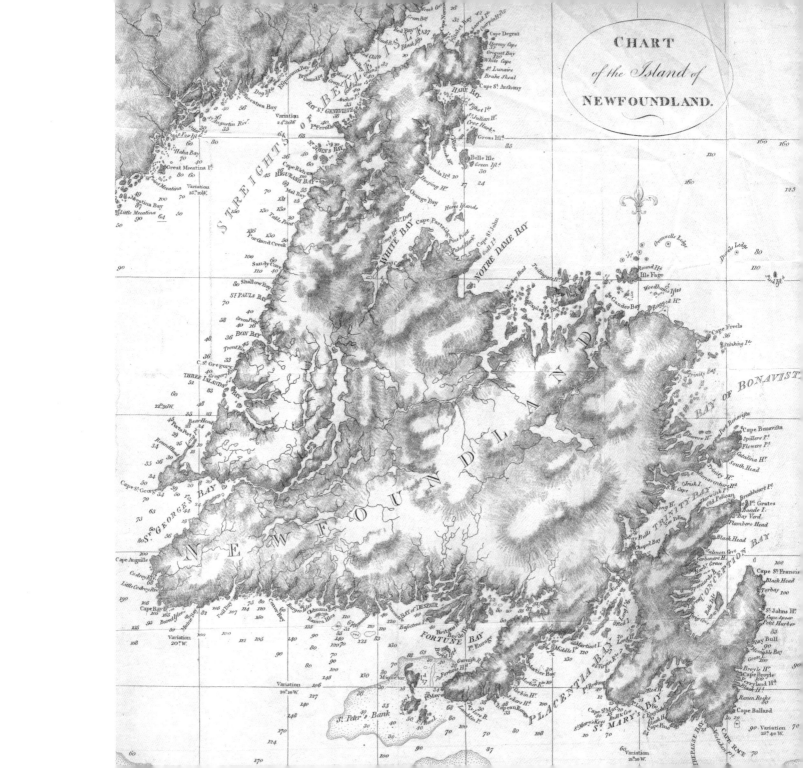

CHART
of the Island of
NEWFOUNDLAND.

At the Shallow Bay campsite in Gros Morne, Rosie and I lug firewood out of her trunk, puzzle together tent poles, anchor pegs in thin soil. Our friends Kim, Adam, and Shelley arrive from Corner Brook. Kim's brought her dog, Trilobite, and we all head down to the water before it gets dark. Coldness bites at our ankles, gradually relaxing its grip. We wade out, farther out, then farther still, surprised to feel mud between our toes even though we can hardly make out our sandals on the beach. Shallow Bay lives up to its name.

Trilo splashes from person to person, checking to see if any of us need rescuing. It's been a while since I've swum in salt water, and I'd forgotten how it lifts you up. We're more buoyant even than the sun, which sinks into the horizon. I can't see my friends against the glare and it feels as if I'm talking to a glowing orange ball of light. The bay turns molten gold. I beeline back to shore for my camera, but my cold hands can't seem to manipulate it into capturing the way the colour solders itself onto my optic nerve.

etween 1857 and 1861, Miot made five voyages to Newfoundland as a French naval officer aboard the *Ardent*, the *Sésostris*, and the *Milan*. His captain, Georges-Charles Cloué, had already spent several seasons charting the island's coastline. Miot and Cloué likely met in 1855 during the Crimean War, and would become lifelong collaborators.

Miot was new to photography, but his skills soon proved invaluable to Cloué's hydrographic work. During their first voyage together, Cloué praised Miot in a letter to Louis Mazères, commodore of the Newfoundland station. "One of the officers of the *Ardent*, Lieutenant Miot,

St. John's taken from Signal Hill, Paul-Émile Miot.

took up photography during his last period of leave," he wrote. "I have given some thought to utilizing this new science, which, until now, might have appeared to have no more than an artistic side, for our precision work, and I believe that, thanks to the ability and the intelligence of Mr. Miot, I have achieved results that give extremely high hopes for the future." Cloué gives some technical details about the surveying process, then continues:

In spite of the difficulties encountered on board in setting up a small, suitably-equipped photographic laboratory, Mr. Miot has succeeded in producing photographs of harbour entrances which offer the highest promise of what this highly-skilled officer could produce with an instrument that has a powerful lens and if he were not frequently halted by an inadequate supply of chemicals.

The camera on board is the property of Mr. Miot. This young, intelligent officer placed it and all of his chemical supplies entirely at my disposal for all of the experiments that I wished to attempt. I made frequent use of them, always with Mr. Miot; for, since I am not a photographer myself, I could not have achieved anything without him.

The last sliver of sun suddenly vanishes, a bright coin dropped into a jukebox, and is replaced by the moon's lopsided grin. Back at our campsite, we build a fire and break out beer and gin, corn on the cob, moose sausages. We toast our toes and take turns feeding the fire stories. Collectively, we've seen great horned owls, great white sharks, giant water bugs. We've pilfered caribou antlers from the Starlite Trail, caught the last boat to Gaultois. Handsome strangers have offered us gum on airplanes. Adam has been to 785 communities in Newfoundland, and Shelley has travelled on every provincial ferry. The fire flares appreciatively.

Inscriptions in rocks near Croque.
Photo by Adam Durocher

Later, Adam will send me a photo he took near Croque, where French sailors carved the names of their ports and ships into the rocks: *1868 Pomone, 1869 Roland*. The solemn glyphs are reminiscent of the Album Rock lettering, but Miot's ships don't seem to be among the names. Miot certainly visited Croque—one of his photos, showing men panning for gold in a river, is believed to have been made near there—but the dates carved into the rocks are all about a decade after his expeditions.

I imagine Miot sitting with us around the fire. He keeps to himself, quietly warming his hands. He has a habit of turning his head toward the sound of the waves.

When you stare at a sunset or a fire and then look away, a lingering afterimage transforms the colours of other things. Miot's strange photograph has this effect on me. All day it's floated before my eyes, flickering over the landscape outside the car windows, steeped sepia by the Shallow Bay sun, projected by the headlamp I wear in the tent. When I close my eyes, it gleams in the darkness like something shiny at the bottom of a pond.

I fall asleep listening to the fire, Miot rustles off through the trees. Tomorrow Rosie and I will continue to Ship Cove.

Vue du Capitaine Georges-Charles Cloué sur le pont du navire l'Ardent (View of Captain Georges-Charles Cloué on the deck of the Ardent), Paul-Émile Miot.

"It would be desirable," Cloué concludes his 1857 letter to Mazères, "for this officer to come to Paris to keep up to date with the advances that have doubtless been made in photography over the past year." Miot did so. In Paris he took steps to establish a photographic atelier at the Dépôt des Cartes et Plans de la Marine, and he joined the Société Française de Photographie in 1858, just one month before setting out on his second voyage to Newfoundland.

21 Juin 1887.
Près de l'Ile Kirpon.

In addition to using his camera to assist in hydrographic work, Miot was called upon to document the French migratory cod fishery. One of his tasks was to produce evidence of British intrusion into areas where the French claimed exclusive rights. In the course of these duties, Miot made some of the earliest photographs of Newfoundland, Cape Breton, and St-Pierre and Miquelon. Many of his albumen prints are now part of the Library and Archives Canada collection, including *Album Rock*.

As *Album Rock* demonstrates, Miot's interest in photography extended beyond the practical and professional. His early travel photos are glimpses of an artist wrestling with a new medium, a new visual vocabulary.

Près de l'île Kirpon (Near Kirpon Island),
Louis Koenig.

"Paul-Émile Miot was not only a draftsman and hydrographer," writes biographer Yves Leroy. "Since 1851, he regularly sent sketches to the newspaper *L'Illustration*. And, from the first campaign in Newfoundland in 1857, he photographed the fisheries of the French Shore. On his return … he confided that he wanted to collect these prints in an *Album of Newfoundland*, whose cover was to be the photograph of a huge rock in Sacred Bay on which the sailors of the *Ardent* had painted the word *Album* in large white letters."

Leroy implies that *Album Rock* was made in 1857, but Library and Archives Canada is less certain, dating it 1857–1859. In 1858, when Miot made his second voyage aboard the *Sésostris*, the Naval Division of Newfoundland was captained by Camille Clément, Baron de La Roncière Le Noury. Although La Roncière travelled aboard a different vessel, the *Gassendi*, his letters to his wife and daughter give us occasional glimpses of Miot's ship.

Near Quirpon.

"I intended to enter Kirpon [Quirpon] but the entrance to the harbour was entirely blocked by ice," he writes of June 20, 1858, "and the *Sésostris* was therefore blocked there." La Roncière's next letter notes that the ships had been trapped for 12 days.

A chunk of ice is visible in the background of Miot's *Album Rock* photo, and I wonder if the photographer was simply amusing himself while his ship was stuck. Still, it's difficult to imagine any officer impressing upon his men the necessity of painting a massive word on a boulder. Surely the supplies on French naval ships were not earmarked for large-scale graffiti projects. Would Miot have had difficulty scrounging up paint, commandeering buckets and ladders, borrowing mops to use as improbable paintbrushes?

This mysterious provenance is what I love about the photograph, all its possible backstories. Historical photography so often preserves visions of industry or ceremony, much less often moments of idle whimsy. There is a kind of magic realism in the scene. It's as if Miot managed, somehow, to photograph a daydream.

Fabrication de l'huile de foie de morue à Terre-Neuve (Making cod liver oil in Newfoundland), Paul-Émile Miot.

Making Cod Liver Oil

After Paul-Émile Miot's *Fabrication de l'huile de morue à Terre-Neuve* (1857)

There's no *make* in making
cod liver oil. It's a god-given thing—
bring a good barrel, slop cod livers in,
let god do the rotting. But *tabarnak,*
it doesn't go any faster if you stand there
staring down the barrel of a strange cannon
wielded by an imbecile who claims it can make
a picture of your face. If I wanted my likeness
sketched, it wouldn't be when it was splattered
with blood and guts, and why should I trust
his glass-eyed blunderbuss not to
blast a hole through my chest? But the idiot's
an officer, so the cod rots in the cold air
while we lean on rancid barrels, on our rifles,

on ladders, Miot slotting us around like
backgammon checkers. *Imagine standing*
before a mirror, he yatters, *and stepping away*
to find your reflection still shimmering
in its frame! Someone asks if his magic mirror
can duplicate women, and Miot hides his grin
behind his contraption. *Hold still,* he says,
blabbering on about glass plates, albumen,
measuring sunlight by the teaspoon. One glance
at the water behind us, tarnished silver
after the storm, is all I need to be certain
no reflection holds still for long. Miot retreats
to his heated cabin, and we get back
to slinging livers. How many months
will my face rot in his tiny barrel
before he skims it off on a sheet of paper?

In Shallow Bay, I wake to the sound of Trilo wuffing as a woodpecker chisels its name into a tree. After a quick breakfast, Rosie and I pack up the car and say goodbye to our friends, who are heading back to Corner Brook.

Neither of us has been up the Northern Peninsula in years. The trees get smaller and farther apart as we drive north, but wildflowers are no less numerous. "It's so pretty," Shelley had remarked yesterday, "but the prettiest places are the worst driving in the winter." As we barrel along the low coastal road, so easily wind-swept, it's not hard to imagine the colours of early summer draining away into black ice and whiteouts.

Rosie's phone rings and she pulls the car over. The shoulder slants sharply down to a rocky beach, and I get out to explore. The beach stones are like flat tongues, each babbling a different language. Bleached crab claws lie mute like broken teeth. I turn over a flat stone and small isopods scatter. I kick at a chunk of shale until the rock splits along its grain. I split slab after slab, the trilobite fossil skulking under the grey stone of my brain.

The longer I look at the *Album Rock* photograph, the more it starts to feel like a page from *Where's Waldo* or *I Spy: A Book of Picture Riddles*. When I first came across the tiny image online I counted two figures: the man silhouetted prominently at the top of the rock, and a second man standing above a short ladder, his white shirt easily mistaken for a punctuation mark as he embellishes the letter *M*. It was only later that I noticed a third sailor lurking beneath the *L*, barely visible except for his collar and a pale staff.

Scratches and faded edges obscure parts of the picture, and it wasn't until I obtained a high-resolution scan from Library and Archives Canada that a fourth figure emerged. The scan was more than 50 times larger than the images I'd found on the web. It was a revelation, like turning a backwards telescope the right way around. What I'd assumed was a spill of paint below the letters metamorphosed into a mop held in a lap. Perfectly camouflaged against the rock, the fourth sailor perches cross-legged below the *M*, staring straight at Miot. A jagged tear in the print jabs him like a lightning bolt.

After a brief stop in St. Anthony, Rosie and I tackle the bumpy road to Ship Cove. Intending to drive into the community to ask about the rock, we're surprised to come across a painted wooden sign marking *Album Rock Trail*, shortly after the turnoff. A steep staircase leads from the roadside down to the water, and we emerge from the treeline to spot Album Rock waiting for us, a prominent boulder looming some distance down the beach. The rock would be a landmark even if Miot had never alighted here—it dominates the shoreline, especially on such a clear, sunny day.

In homage or in jest, someone has neatly spray-painted the word *Album* in white letters on the side of the rock facing us. Rounding the outcrop, I'm relieved to find Miot's original canvas untouched, and surprised at the presence of a gazebo beside the boulder. I had heard there was a display of Miot's photos somewhere in Ship Cove, but I hadn't expected the rock itself to be so well-marked. It must be a recent development—the wooden boards of the gazebo are still unweathered, and there isn't a single name carved into the picnic table.

In Miot's many photos of sailors and officers, I'm drawn to the apparatus of the ship itself. Coils of rope, rigging and pulleys, draped sailcloth. In a photo taken when the *Ardent* was docked in Lorient, France, before its departure for Newfoundland, the ship is a nest of sweeping rope and towering masts, a tangle of vertical and diagonal lines. Men are small dark lumps in the belly of its rickety skeleton. Everything is askew, aslant, akimbo. The *Ardent* was a hybrid steam and sailing ship, and metal pipes jut from the deck. I imagine the heaviness of it all—oiled cloth, timber, coal, cannonballs—and the heaving of the ship at sea, perpetually finding its balance.

Everything in the image *looms*, especially through the sepia fog of the albumen print. And yet somehow this contraption carried Miot across the Atlantic and back. With its wooden framework and interwoven lines, the ship feels like a loom, works like a loom. It takes in wind and a scarf of seafoam unfurls from the other side. It weaves its way.

It's almost unfathomable how much of Miot's life was spent on ships. After leaving Trinidad he attended boarding school in Ireland (where he learned English), then enrolled in the Naval Academy in Paris. First as a naval officer, later as lieutenant and captain, he sailed to the West Indies, the Crimea, Newfoundland and Cape Breton, Mexico, Uruguay, California, Chile, Tahiti and the Marquesas Islands, Tunisia, and Madagascar, before retiring in Paris. He was later made curator of the Musée de la Marine at the Louvre. One naval historian calculated that Miot had clocked 298 months (nearly 25 years) of maritime navigation in his 50-year career.

Sur le pont du navire l'Ardent avant son départ (On the deck of the ship Ardent before its departure), Paul-Émile Miot.

Captain, photographer, curator, graffiti artist, and seemingly part albatross. But what sort of person was Miot? Much of the biographical information I'd found came from a website set up by Michael Wilkshire, a retired Memorial University historian who has extensively researched Newfoundland's French Shore. I email Michael asking to meet, hoping that Miot and I can be more formally introduced.

In Sacred Bay, beside the gazebo, a wooden panel displays a reproduction of the *Album Rock* photograph. "Where was the 19th-century photographer standing when he took this picture?" it asks. "Find the spot!" I oblige, circumnavigating the gazebo while comparing my view with an image on my phone. Strangely, it looks as if Miot must have been standing much higher than I am, perhaps on the gazebo's roof—but his ship could not have sailed this far in. From here I can easily see, however, where his sailors must have stood while painting. The bottom of the rock forms a partial ledge, but a ladder would have been needed to reach the *M*.

Rosie clambers to the top, and I follow her up. We've a fine view. The tide is out, and the cove's blue mirror is broken only by undulating patches of orange kelp. In the distance, the houses and outbuildings of Ship Cove are flecks of white paint. The trees jutting from the top of Miot's rock are long gone, and we sit cross-legged on soft moss. We take turns posing like French sailors, hands on chins. We jump down again.

Someone has hammered a piece of rebar into the very top of the rock. Someone has smashed a beer bottle at its base. Scouring the rock face for unlikely traces of painted letters, we find only minuscule fireworks of white and orange lichen, exploding their slow rings. How long does lichen live? Can time be measured in its circles, like the inside of a tree? How many lichen rings away is Miot?

I want to photograph my meeting with Michael Wilkshire—steam rising from two mugs of tea, condensation on coffee shop windows, Michael's wispy eyebrows—but I settle for writing things down. Michael's brought me copies of two *Newfoundland Quarterly* articles that he and archaeologist Gerald Penney wrote about Miot, and we chat a little about the *Album Rock* photo. Michael's familiar with the image, although he's only seen smaller reproductions.

I bring up the high-resolution scan on my laptop, and we zoom in on the sailors. Their hands and faces are distinctly darker in tone than the rock's dark surface, and I'm curious about their identity. In all likelihood they are white French sailors, but based on the tones of the photograph, I'd guess they were people of colour. Michael tells me that Miot's naval unit travelled between Newfoundland and the West Indies. They might have picked up crew in the Caribbean, but it's more likely I'm misreading murky pixels and suntanned skin.

Album Rock is a portrait of a place, but also of a group of people, and their anonymity complicates the image. The men are just far enough from the camera that their facial expressions are out of reach, and I wish there was some way to get closer. Is that blurry squiggle a smirk, or a smile? Is the photograph a playfully staged bit of theatre, something Miot suggested on a lark to occupy idle crewmen? Or were the sailors ordered to paint and pose, perhaps resentful of wasting time and resources on such a frivolous act, so far from home?

Ship Cove's pocket of ocean is nestled within the larger embrace of Sacred Bay. From the top of the rock I can't see the entrance to the bay, and the cove seems entirely surrounded by low hills, like a lake. On such a calm day it's an undeniably beautiful place. Curiosity brought me here, and mosquitos are inquisitive about me in return. Other than Rosie and me, the only visitors are a family having a beach fire near the bottom of the trailhead stairs, far away down the curving shoreline. A child's laugh skips across the water. Rosie curls up on a nearby boulder with a book, while I take photos and write in the gazebo.

White lichen, spattered across the rock face where *Album* was written, looks tantalizingly like paint. I've brought a macro lens and make close-up photos of the tiny crustose forms. In a crevice where the *B* in *Album* would have been, I notice a different patch of white that might be dead lichen, or something else. Most of the lichen is orange, and decidedly not 160-year-old paint. There shouldn't be paint, there's no way there could still be paint, but I can't help but look. The rock's surface feels fragile, crumbly, a rough grey with seams of quartz. The ledge is speckled with bird droppings that are also not paint.

Stepping back, I compare Miot's photo with the landscape before me. A tree that once bristled from the rock is now a wizened stump, its bent limbs reminiscent of Miot's posing sailor. It's only now, visiting the site, that I realize the figure on the rock would have been gazing at a forested hillside, not the ocean. With his hand shading his eyes, I had pictured him surveying the sea, as if looking out from a crow's nest. Perhaps this is a bit of artifice, Miot manipulating the scene—or perhaps it was the island, not the Atlantic, that felt unknown to the sailors.

Maggoty Biscuit

Not every godforsaken rock
needs a name. If it's the first glimpse of land
you've had in thirty days, if it's gargantuan or
misshapen, if you startled a devil or an angel
in its shadow, or left a friend sleeping there
in a makeshift grave, then sure. Otherwise,
leave it for lichen to squabble over. What use are landmarks
anyway, in a place where any birdshit-stained boulder
is as good as the next? If you wanted to find this one again
you'd just search Sacred Bay for a massive cannonball
smashed off the hill and collapsed into slag. A slug of turf
crawling out to sea in hopes of becoming an island.
A big maggoty biscuit—now there's a name for it.

Maggoty Biscuit. One Last Tooth. Burnt Boot.
Miot's Stone Boat. You'd be surprised how soon
you run out of namesakes—after the usual saints
and superior officers, a half-dozen ancestors,
a hometown, maybe the first ship you sailed on,
what's left in a sailor's life that's familiar enough
to be written in stone? It doesn't take long
before you're naming boulders after bad dreams,
after any skipper who didn't get you maimed, after the cat
that skulked around that tavern in Calais. In any case,
the captain'd sooner write *Baie sans nom* on his map
than ask for my suggestions. But I've got
maps of my own. I can close my eyes and see
every knot and dent in this ship, its every
bolt and barnacle, as clearly as the sky displays
Grande Ourse, Andromède, Cassiopée.

Retour du beau temps (The return of pleasant weather), Louis Koenig.

Marins français dans les rochers (French sailors climbing rocks), Paul-Émile Miot.

Miot's keen eye for composition is evident in all his photos, but his subjects are usually conventional maritime fare: tall ships, townscapes, officers leaning on bulwarks. I ask Michael if he's come across any others as whimsical as *Rocher peint par les marins français*. "Yes, there is one," he says, and produces a thick binder from his bag. It's full of reproductions of albumen prints from various collections. He opens it to a certain page.

The photograph, captioned *Marins français dans les rochers*, was also taken in Newfoundland, and is in many ways similar to *Album Rock*. Four sailors gambol on a rocky coastline, the water behind them scattered with chunks of ice. The horizon has the same tilt. Two men are reaching down to a third, offering hands and rope in a contrived manner. A fourth lounges beside them, one foot firmly conquering a stone. Is this the same individual standing atop Album Rock? Could the same four sailors have posed for both pictures? It's possible, Michael tells me, although the exact location of this photo isn't known, and both photos are dated 1857–1859.

Looking closely at *Album Rock* and then *Marins français*, I want the dark triangle to the left of Album Rock to match the distinctly pyramidal rock in the climbing photo. It doesn't. But the photos do share a certain theatricality, the same sense of the rugged landscape as a stage. With the photos side by side, it's easy to imagine them as two scenes from the same play, with the same cast of actors.

Miot crossed an ocean to end up here. I've merely travelled from one corner of an island to another, but I still feel unfamiliar with this place. I haven't spent much time on the Northern Peninsula, and I'm not here long enough to get acquainted. It's a quick trip, just a taste of the place, and I feel a little parasitic, like a mosquito drawing blood.

But I take in the air, touch the water, watch the light change. I spend time in the presence of the rock, press my hands against its surface, gaze out from its crow's nest, and perhaps this is enough. Standing on the rock, I try to picture the *Ardent* or *Sésostris* anchored in the vast bay, twin masts and smokestack mirrored in the blue. There's so much I don't know. What time of year was Miot here? A growler of ice in the background of *Album Rock* suggests spring, and another of Miot's photos showing ice floes in Sacred Bay might be from the same voyage.

Rosie and I leave the rock to the early evening light and drive to nearby St. Lunaire-Griquet. We check in at St. Brendan's Motel, indulge in deep-fried ice cream, and walk to the ocean's edge. Sunset is noticeably later than we're used to, and at first I think it's because we're farther north, then realize it's that we're on the west side of the time zone. The beach is a ridge of shale with its knife edge upwards, littered with innumerable tiny vertebrae and rusted bits of metal. It's so, so quiet. Like the flotsam, we come to the water to be disassembled.

What can I learn by simply studying Miot's photo? Looking closely, it occurs to me that *Album Rock* has a curious relationship with scale. At first glance, I read the rock as much less massive, covered in shrubs, and the letters graffitied by a single hand. It's only when I notice the figure silhouetted above the rock that everything shifts to its proper magnitude. The shrubs grow into stubby, windblown trees, the letters stand as tall as the sailor, and gradually the other men step from the shadows, one by one.

The sailor at the bottom left holds a long staff, perhaps a measuring device. It looks about the same height as the letters, and when I zoom in I can make out markings along its length. You'd surely need some kind

of ruler to plot stems and serifs so precisely on an uneven surface. Beside the same man there's another stick propped on the rock, and a shapeless blob that must be a blanket or cloth. There are so many details in the image that I can't quite decipher.

I perceive the pale sky of *Album Rock* as overcast, a sheet of white. But it might very well have been a patchwork of clouds. "Most nineteenth-century photographic emulsions are blue-sensitive and hence cannot record the sky—overcast, partially cloudy, and sunny skies are all overexposed," explains Errol Morris in *Believing Is Seeing: Observations on the Mysteries of Photography*. "The sky is a featureless white, but the 'whiteness' of the sky is unrelated to the question of whether there are clouds or whether you can see shadows. It was only much later that panchromatic film—film that was less blue-sensitive—was developed."

The lighting in the photograph is consistent with the cloudy skies of coastal Newfoundland—there are no glimmers on the water, no shadows under the ladder. Still, I can't help but wonder what else I'm missing when I look at the image. Mostly, I wish I could push the edges of the frame outwards, expand the panorama, so I might catch a glimpse of a ship in the harbour, or the elusive photographer.

Miot Cove (in St. John Bay) and Miot Point (in Bide Arm), two minor landmarks on the French Shore, are probably named after the photographer. Miot presumably didn't intend to name Album Rock, but the toponym has stuck. Looking at the photo, I have to remind myself that the word *album* is written in French, not English (although Miot was fluent in both). Even though *album* has the same meaning in both languages, the distinction feels important. French place names linger around the coastline of Newfoundland even in places where the language is no longer spoken, their meaning and pronunciation evolving over generations. The *B. du Désespoir* (Bay of Despair)

Aspect de glaces, près du Kirpon (*Views of ice, near Kirpon*), Louis Koenig.

Baie du Kinfson   21 Juin 89

Espace des îles blanches

shown on a 1744 French map eventually became known as *Bay d'Espoir* (Bay of Hope), which to English ears relapses back to "despair." And, of course, colonial British and French place names have overwritten indigenous names. Ktaqamkuk, Terre-Neuve, Newfoundland. Every map is a palimpsest.

Another of Miot's photos is captioned *Iceberg dans la baie de Kirpon*. Like *Album Rock* and *Marins français*, it shows a group of sailors posing before an icy seascape. But the people here are mostly superfluous, as Miot's subject is clearly the gigantic iceberg hulking in the bay. It's that species of iceberg that's more *site* than *sight*, a strange island too fickle to be named.

Before leaving the Northern Peninsula, Rosie and I visit Quirpon (pronounced "Kar-poon"). We follow a road until it ends, past houses with their walls caved in but their lawns freshly mowed. Rabbits dart across the road. We park beside a sign marking the way to Lancie Bauld Head, and push through even though the trail is utterly overgrown with alders. Old boardwalks with flaking red paint have been smashed to pieces by the trees, boards cracked and missing. What's left of the path is cobbled in moose droppings.

We almost turn back, but the view is worth the slog—14 icebergs, if we count the smallest ones. Just offshore there's a large island, also called Quirpon, which is considered the northernmost extent of the island of Newfoundland. But when we're back in the car and I pull up Google Maps, the island vanishes, painted

over by bland blue ocean. It doesn't exist on the roadmap, since there are no roads there.

On the drive home, Rosie and I pass a sign for Nameless Cove. How does a place end up with a name like that? The story is that it used to be called Flower's Cove, until the nearby community of French Island Harbour borrowed the name Flower's Cove and didn't give it back, leaving its neighbour nameless. Names around here can be as mercurial as icebergs. What would Album Rock be called today, if Miot had never shown up?

As we go through his album of Miot reproductions, Michael points out intriguing details. There's the freshly built Basilica, dominating the skyline in one of the oldest photographs of St. John's. There's a charming portrait labelled "Captain L"—Michael tells me that someone once emailed him to ask if the captain might be her grandfather. He shows me the peculiar paddle-wheel housing on the hybrid sail and steam ships, and Miot's photo of fishing stages which could be tilted to better catch the sun. He points out woodchips carpeting the ground around a Mi'kmaq tent.

Michael has also brought some negatives in an envelope labelled *Gobineau*. They're Miot photos that Michael used in his book about Count Joseph Arthur de Gobineau, a French diplomat whom Miot likely encountered in 1859. A member of the Anglo-French Commission mediating France's fishing rights, Gobineau attended a meeting on the *Sésostris* on June 28, 1859. Michael's translation of his writings on Newfoundland is titled *A Gentleman in the Outports*, but Gobineau is an undeniably sinister figure. His infamous *Essay on the Inequality of Human Races* was published in 1855, and he is mostly remembered for his attempts to legitimize racism through pseudoscience.

Portrait d'un marin pris à bord du navire l'Ardent (Portrait of a sailor taken on board the Ardent), Paul-Émile Miot. Michael Wilkshire notes that a similar print in the Bibliothèque nationale is captioned "Captain L., one of the ablest fishermen on the coast of Newfoundland."

Avisos à roues au mouillage, Nord de Terre-Neuve (Moored avisos, Northern Newfoundland),
Paul-Émile Miot

Gobineau had been sent to Newfoundland as punishment, having refused a post in Beijing on the grounds that it was no place for a "civilized European." He hated the island, complaining in letters that "[t]his is an awful country. It is very cold, there is almost constant fog, and one sails between pieces of floating ice of enormous size."

If the story of Miot in Newfoundland needed a villain, Gobineau would be the obvious candidate. His bigotry is on clear display when he writes of encountering Mi'kmaq people in Cape Breton en route to the island. Around the same time, Miot made several portraits of Mi'kmaq men and women, sometimes posed on the deck of the *Sésostris*. Most are presented respectfully, but there's a disquieting series of prints showing the same Mi'kmaq woman first fully dressed, then exposing a single breast, then bare-chested. She looks unmistakably suspicious, distrustful, exasperated. Another woman is photographed in a similar manner. One of the more lurid images was later used to illustrate Gobineau's *Voyage à Terre-Neuve*.

Michael and I hold his negatives up to the window to illuminate the miniature landscapes. So much of this research involves looking beyond photography in search of a bigger picture. How can I get closer to Miot? I suppose his skeleton is buried somewhere, but whatever's left of his brain is scattered throughout various archives in France. Michael has done a lot of that research, and I'm lucky to have his translations.

I can't go to Paris, but I'll be in Ottawa in a few weeks, and a curator at the National Gallery has agreed to meet with me.

Middle of Nowhere?

No, but if you split nowhere down the middle
like a cod, you could say the place where we landed
was its noggin, cut off and thrown to the lobsters.
The jowls of nowhere. Of course, to Miot
the wretched rock was a delicacy, a cod tongue
floured and fried in butter and onions.
Plenty of kindling at least, and he let us have a fire
like it was some grand gesture. We roasted potatoes
and he circled the rock, over and over,
as if ogling Amiens Cathedral. I pissed on a tree
for the first time in three weeks. Next morning
Miot had us rowing back with a ladder, rope and mops,
a bucket of whitewash, and a broomstick
fashioned into a kind of ruler. He traced five letters
in the mud, insisted we copy them *juste comme ça,*
dressed in their prissiest. I've never felt so foolish
as when propping that ladder against his shabby boulder,

slathering a giant *A* on the backside of a rock
like we're christening a ship, as if afterwards we'll smash a bottle
against its bow, sail off into sunset. I dipped a mop
in the lime mixture and wondered how far it would fit
up Miot's nose. But a spirited breeze soon shooed the mosquitos,
and within thirty minutes it had split and salted my brain
so I felt I could paint all afternoon. All four of us
settled in to the work. We started whistling, even.
The smell of earth, the sun glinting off slob ice and off Miot's lens
as he took aim at us from a safe distance,
as if we were some new species of songbird
and he was trying to figure out what to name us.

The National Gallery's curatorial wing has high security. "Is this a meeting, or just a visit?" asks the guard at the entrance, and for a moment I'm not sure how to answer. The guard takes my ID and makes a phone call, and presently I'm escorted to a long, quiet room with tall windows overlooking the Ottawa River. One wall is lined with shallow shelves for displaying artwork and documents.

Lori Pauli, the National Gallery's Curator of Photographs, shakes my hand warmly. She's brought a cart with three cases of Miot prints and has taken out some photos from Chile and Uruguay. We look at them together. Lori explains that her specialty is 19th-century Canadian and European photos, and that she's acquired some of Miot's prints from a collector in Germany. Library and Archives Canada has a separate collection, and she tries not to duplicate what they have.

Opening a metal case to reveal a hefty photographic album, Lori removes her white gloves. "They get in the way sometimes," she says. As she carefully turns the pages of the album, full of Miot's dreamlike images of Tahitian landscapes and people, Lori tells me that Miot trained as a painter and that this might explain the wonderful composition of so many of his photographs. She notes that Miot's photos of Tahiti and the Marquesas Islands, which were frequently used by other artists as references, might have influenced Paul Gauguin's decision to travel there.

Femme Mi'kmaq à bord du navire Sésostris (Mi'kmaq woman on board the Sésostris), Paul-Émile Miot.

While Gauguin famously painted Tahiti as a lush paradise full of women bearing flowers and fruit, Miot's photographs of the place and people are more subdued and stark. For the most part, both men portray their indigenous Tahitian subjects with serenity and gravitas, although they also share the same troubling colonialist gaze. Gauguin undresses and romanticizes the islanders, while Miot's images sometimes come across more as ethnographic documents than portraits. This is certainly true of Miot's Mi'kmaq portraits as well. "There is a notable lack of ease on the part of Miot's Mi'kmaw sitters, probably reflecting the social and cultural distance between a French naval officer and his subjects," observes curator Edward Tompkins.

While Lori and I are talking, I can't help glancing at the river through the tall windows. A hawk pivots in mid-air and arcs downwards to the water, which glints with late afternoon light. A black squirrel ripples along a banister.

I had thought that Library and Archives Canada's collection was also housed at the National Gallery, but Lori tells me it's across the river, in Gatineau. The physical print of *Album Rock* is there, and Lori insists that I see it, even though tomorrow is my last day in Ottawa. She calls an associate at the Archives to set up a viewing. They usually require a few days' notice, so this is very last-minute, but someone agrees to retrieve the print for me.

When Jerry Evans and I look at some of Miot's Tahitian portraits together, Jerry leans close to the screen. "I'm looking for tattoos," he says. Traditional hand-poked tattooing has become part of Jerry's art practice, which includes printmaking, painting, and filmmaking. We meet at St. Michael's Printshop, where he's working on some new prints.

In the 1990s, Jerry used photocopy transfers to include some of Miot's Mi'kmaq photos in a series of lithographs. In prints such as *Mi'kmaq Women of the French Shore* and *We Were Not the Savages*, the artist surrounds Miot's photos with his own imagery, reclaiming them as part of his own ancestry and visual culture. The colourful lithographs interrogate Miot's images, alternatingly drawing attention to the women's plight and placing feathers as if to shield them.

Jerry remembers first encountering the Mi'kmaq photos through archaeologist Gerald Penney, who had come across them in an archive. "When those photos were rediscovered," Jerry tells me, "it was a big deal. There were articles about them in *The Telegram*, and Peter Gzowski talked about them on CBC Radio. But in the newspaper and on the radio, they never talked about the photos with the women half-undressed," he says. "And you can see in the expression on their faces, they don't look too happy. So I wanted to draw attention to that."

We Were Not the Savages, Jerry Evans, 1998.

"We Were Not The Savages"   6/7   J. Evans 98

Jerry reminds me that the Mi'kmaq were allied with the French, and the women would likely have spoken French. *Mi'kmaq* may have originated from a word meaning *friend*. We chat about the contrast between some of Miot's other Mi'kmaq portraits, which show their subjects in more dignified, classical poses, and the harshly exploitative photos of the two women.

Later, I'm reminded of our discussion while reading Susan Sontag's essay about traumatic photographs, *Regarding the Pain of Others*. "The other," writes Sontag, "even when not an enemy, is regarded only as someone to be seen, not someone (like us) who also sees." It's evident from his photographs that Miot sees his Mi'kmaq and Tahitian subjects not as individuals but as types, as specimens. The captions of his portraits of French officers always identify the sitter, but his subjects from other cultures, for the most part, remain nameless.

The National Archives Preservation Centre in Gatineau is a vast glass façade enclosing a concrete bunker. Samantha Shields meets me in the lobby. She gives me a short tour of a labyrinth of cubicles and moveable walls, explaining that the working area is designed to be reconfigurable to accommodate large artifacts. The building is hushed, like a library, and the air feels very clean. We pass doors labelled Film Preservation and Mould Abatement.

Samantha takes me to a small room with a wide table. A security camera is aimed at the table, which contains a pair of cotton gloves and sheet of paper that says *Caution: Artifact Below*. Beneath it, in a clear plastic sleeve, is the print of *Album Rock*, about the size of a *National Geographic* magazine. Fluorescent lights reflecting in the plastic make the landscape shimmer. In this architectural marvel of metal and glass, the yellowed paper looks so out of place, out of time.

Encountering the print as a physical object helps me understand the imperfections in the scanned image. Aside from a long tear that has been repaired with archivist's tape, the print itself is in relatively good shape. The damaged corners and edges of the image are from distress to the original negative. Samantha

says that although the print shows the full glass plate, it would have been cropped when mounted in an album. I mention that I'm puzzled by the tilted horizon—the photo is otherwise so thoughtfully composed that it seems odd. I wonder if it might have been to make the word *Album* more level.

With my macro lens, I snap close-ups of the four sailors, the five letters, and a few other details. Fibres in the paper catch the light and show up as bright lines. Samantha has brought two boxes of other prints by Miot, and I photograph the climbing photo (*Marins français dans les rochers*) as well.

Later, squinting at paper fibres and silver grains in the magnified photos, I wish I could say I solved the puzzle of whether the same four individuals appear in both images, or discovered some clue to the identity of the men. But mostly it reminds me of looking for traces of paint on the rock—murky, muddled shapes that don't yield any details I didn't already know.

The only way to make the picture clearer might be to track down the original negative in Paris. Unfortunately, Michael Wilkshire informs me that it was almost certainly destroyed, like many of Miot's glass plates, by a World War II bomb.

Michael is eager to hear about my progress in chipping away at *Album Rock*. We first met in July, and by the time we get together again, the sidewalks are slick with ice. I show Michael the photos I took in Sacred Bay and tell him about my trip to Ottawa. Sometimes it feels as if I'm running in circles, chasing Miot as he hides on the other side of the rock, the other side of the camera. His photos show me the world through his eyes, but I can only imagine what he's thinking, what kind of person he might have been.

It would be different if Miot had left a journal, or letters. The only hint of his voice is the preface to a book titled *La Marine d'Autrefois* (*The Navy of Yesteryear*) by Georges Contesse, which Miot wrote while curator of the Musée de la Marine at the Louvre. Published in 1897, it's an eccentric collage of old and new. "Soon we shall go under the sea," proclaims Miot, "laughing at the tumultuousness of the surface; soon, the fastest ships will be outpaced by astonishing vehicles rolling like locomotives over the waves." But his zest for the future is tempered by wistfulness. "How many people know the most beautiful lighthouse in the world," he writes, "is that of Cordouan?"

The closest I have to a written account of Miot's time in Newfoundland is Cloué's letter to Mazères, in which he praises Miot's initiative and ingenuity. Michael warns me that Cloué might not be the most objective character reference. "Remember," Michael says, "Cloué was Miot's great protector." The two men sailed halfway around the globe together and both rose to great distinction in the French navy.

Trawling through various historical accounts, I sometimes get tantalizingly close to Miot. He almost shows up in the *Evening Telegram* on July 24, 1860, when a massive ceremony was held in St. John's to mark the official landing of Albert Edward (Edward VII), Prince of Wales. The *Telegram* reports: "His Royal Highness was about to leave the ship for the shore, and the salutes from the muzzles of the *Ariadne*, *Hero*, *Flying Fish*, *Sésostris*, and the land batteries, were followed by such enthusiastic cheers from the throats of the congregated thousands on the shore as to make the old hills resound with the joyful shouts." A contemporary account by Robert Cellem describes the after-party a few days later: "Among the company assembled were the officers of the different ships in port, dressed in full uniform; the officers of the Royal Newfoundland corps, and of the French ship, the *Sésostris*, together with a plentiful sprinkling of gentlemen belonging to the militia—all contributing to lend additional *gaiety* and brilliance to the scene."

If only someone on Miot's ship had kept a diary. "There might be someone," Michael muses. "A sailor named Scias, who sailed with Miot. A distant relative of Scias contacted me through the Miot website, years ago. And there's a journal. If I remember correctly, Scias writes disparagingly of both Miot and Cloué. They're sailing somewhere in South America, I think Chile. France and Britain were at war at the time, so the French sometimes went privateering, collecting 'prizes' from British ships they waylaid. Anything they won would be divvied up amongst the men. And Scias," Michael continues, "wrote that Cloué was a bit of a scaredy-cat, that he didn't have the guts to go after prizes. And he mentions that they were exploring, hiking somewhere, and that Miot was moaning about having to get his feet wet!"

The journal is in French, of course, but Michael promises to dig it out of his files and send me translations of the juicy bits.

I mention that I've been reading about how the sky is often blank in old landscape photos, because film didn't register the colour blue. Michael tells me that there's a similar effect that happens with early photographic portraits, since it could take a few minutes to make an exposure. People would lean into specially built braces to help them stand still for the camera. But they couldn't help but glance around the room, and the movement of their eyes shows up as a spooky white blur, as if they have no pupils at all.

Close-up of Album Rock on Cloué's *Baie du Sacre* map.

In the satellite images on Google Maps, Album Rock appears as a bright oblong shape just touching shore, as if it's a boat docked in Sacred Bay. Just to the northeast, on Great Sacred Island, a similarly sized blob is the wreck of the SS *Langleecrag*, which ran aground in 1947. The ship's rusting hulk, which from the mainland looks like an enormous orange boulder, puzzles many visitors to L'Anse aux Meadows.

I've been wondering if Album Rock shows up on Cloué's navigational charts, and decide to investigate. At The Rooms Archives, I take over two long tables. An archivist brings out a pair of oversized folders full of maps from the French Hydrographic Charts collection. I've requested No. 1704, *Baie du Sacre (Côte Nord de Terre-Neuve)*, and No. 1453, *Côte Nord de Terre-Neuve comprise entre Le Cap d'Oignon*, dated 1857 and 1854.

At first I don't recognize the strange bays and peninsulas on the *Baie du Sacre* map, then realize I'm mistaking land for water and water for land. I'm used to maps that have a landmass in the middle, but these are nautical charts, centred on bodies of water. Sacred Bay swarms with tiny numbers like schools of fish. The coastline is clustered with islands, and its intricacies are lovingly hand-drawn, with different textures for vegetation, sand, steep hills, sheer cliffs. A few meagre rectangles scattered around Cape Onion are the only hint that anyone lives here. Except for an occasional hill the land is completely empty, and the map feels like a portrait in which the artist has painted every crease and loose thread of someone's clothing but left out the face. Album Rock is an earring, a small sharp oval faceted like a gemstone.

Peering closely at a drawing from Cloué's *Pilote de Terre-Neuve*.

le Kirpon   I.J. Cartier   P.te des Esquimaux   Petite Ile du Sacre   S.E.¼ S à 1 ¼ mille   G.de Ile du Sacre

N° 113. Vue prise à 3 Milles au N.N.E. du Cap d'Oignon.

...quimaux   Cap Corbeau   C. Noir   Cap d'Ardoise   Petite Ile du Sacre   C. d'Artimon

N° 114. Etant à 1 Mille $\frac{3}{4}$ au N. de la P.te N. de la Grande Ile du Sacre.

...doise   Petite Ile du Sacre   C. d'Artimon   Pointe Nord   Grande Ile du Sacre

Suite du N° 114.

Coastline near Sacred Bay, from Cloué's *Pilote de Terre-Neuve*.

I've also requested to look at Cloué's *Pilote de Terre-Neuve*, published in 1869, which consists of two volumes bound in red leather. Both are full of wonderful drawings of coastlines and the entrances to harbours. Miot's photographs would have been used to help make these, and he may have even drawn some of them. They're meant as diagrams, not illustrations, but they're as delightful as any children's book, especially the drawings furnished with buildings and ships like dollhouse furniture. I recognize familiar place names (Le Cap Spear, Gros Morne, Blowmedown), and spend an hour wandering around the coastline with Cloué as my tour guide, marvelling at the island in miniature.

À bord de l'Ibis en tournée sur la côte Est (On board the Ibis touring the east coast), Louis Koenig.

1. Cap d'Oignon 2. Baie du Sacre 3. Baie de Saint-Mein 4. Cap des Epées 5. Hâvre Saint-Antoine
6. Hâvre de la Crémaillière 7. Hâvre des Petites Oies 8. Baie aux Lièvres 9. La Source 10. Hâvre de la Tête-de-Mort 11. Le Capucin 12. Baie du Croc 13. Cap Vent

"I found the Scias journal," Michael emails me, "but unfortunately it's not the one I was remembering. The fellow who sailed with Miot in the Pacific was someone else. It was an unpublished manuscript that a fellow sent me and I can't track it down … I suspect that he is no longer alive."

Like the paper fibres that gleam from my macro photos of the print, my research into *Album Rock* is a mishmash of little loose ends. I keep digging, but it feels as if the bits and pieces I'm uncovering are so trivial it's impossible to piece them into anything.

The web is an endless source of bits and pieces. I find a photo from 1871 attributed to Félix Auguste Le Clerc, who sailed with Miot in the Pacific, and later toured Newfoundland himself. Titled *Prenant un Ris à Bord de L'Astrée*, it shows five sailors teetering dozens of feet above deck, their butts in the air as they presumably fasten something to the mast (see page 104).

I also come across a strange drawing of two men flying on the back of a large bird. One of them peers through a telescope at a hieroglyphic map of the tip of the Northern Peninsula—a drawing of an onion marks Cape Onion, a priest represents Sacred Bay, and a skull denotes a place called *Hâvre de la Tête-de-Mort*. It's captioned "After a drawing found in the albums of Admiral Cloué". Months later I discover the original painting in full colour, part of a marvellous collection of watercolours by Louis Koenig, who accompanied Le Clerc to Newfoundland in 1885.

The archives of the Bibliothèque Nationale de France are especially useful. Michael mentioned that there should be another print of *Album Rock* in their collection, so I search for "Miot" and "Terre-Neuve" and other keywords, scrolling through pages of documents and maps. One of the search results is an album titled *42 phot. de Saint-Pierre et Miquelon, de Cap-Breton, de Terre-Neuve, du Labrador, par Julien Thoulet.* I skim a few pages, curious whether there are any photos from places I recognize.

Suddenly it tumbles from my screen—the gargantuan, unmistakable silhouette of Album Rock. In Thoulet's photo it's farther away, parked like an old car beside the steep, forested hillside. The tall tree on its peak is gone, and the letters … I zoom in on the image, and lean closer to my screen. Most of the rock face is bare, but I can clearly make out the distinct diagonal slash of the letter *A*, just where it should be. Comparing Thoulet's photo more closely with Miot's, I find faint traces of the upper-left of the *L*, a little curve from the *B*, and, barely legible, the middle zag of the *M*. Only the *U* appears to have vanished entirely.

Thoulet's photograph is dated 1886, Miot's about 1857. The painted letters lasted at least 30 years, surviving 30 northern Newfoundland winters. No wonder the name Album Rock stuck. So many people must have stumbled upon the rock and been utterly flummoxed.

Vue 28, from 42 phot. de Saint-Pierre et Miquelon, de Cap-Breton, de Terre-Neuve, du Labrador, Julien Thoulet (BnF).

scratches his initials in the corner of a photograph

as if with a fishhook dipped in an inkwell. Look at how lightly

P peers over the shoulder of E and adjusts its

hat-brim, at how E scratches its chin; how many times

has this hand carved a line into the black slate

of the sea and hauled back white fish

like writhing veins of quartz, or pacified the tremor

of a compass needle in its wooden box? Look how the dot

after P and the dot of i nail the whole assemblage down,

how E is taken aback by what looks like an iron spike

scuttering across the deck, but hasn't realized yet

that it's merely missing its accent. This is the signature

of a man who might misplace the address of his sister in Paris
after three years at sea, but will never forget
the way the sun signed its ten thousand names on the water
as the *Astrée* first lowered its sails in Antofagasta.
Look how *M* arches one eyebrow and curls its moustache
like a cartoon villain—this is the signature of a sailor
who has tossed firecrackers into Tahitian bonfires,
spit in the mouths of maelstroms, who if he'd lived another
hundred years would have laughed his ass off
at *SpongeBob SquarePants*. Look at how *i, o, t*
crowd together, yielding every iota of elbow room
to the capital letters; this is the signature of a hand
bound by chain-of-command, that crosses its chest
nord, sud, est, ouest. Look at the way *t* leans precariously
over a landwash like a salt-blasted snag, the way its bowsprit
sweeps back on itself like a beached wave, and like a wave
ends just where it begins to rise.

Aviso français l'Ardent accosté à une estacade de bois
(French aviso Ardent docked at a wooden pier), Paul-Émile Miot.

When you're a 19th-century photographer and your camera can't record clouds, do you settle for washed-out skies? Of course not! You simply paint the clouds yourself, along with their reflections, as Thoulet has done in his photo titled *Le village de l'Anse à Bois au Kirpon*. When I ask Michael about Thoulet, he tells me that he was a French geologist and oceanographer who spent the 1886 season on board the *Clorinde* (along with Le Clerc and Koenig), and points me toward Thoulet's *A Voyage to Newfoundland*, translated by Memorial University professor Scott Jamieson.

Like his gently retouched photographs, Thoulet's writing is part observation, part embellishment. His incisive descriptions often veer into something closer to storytelling, such as this rumination on how places are named:

> On the map of Newfoundland, Fréhel, Groix, Belle-Isle, St-Lunaire are reminders of the poor Breton sailor preserving the memory of the land of his birth, when he saw resemblances more with his heart than his eyes and gave familiar names to the fog-shrouded capes of these wild islands. The banal names Grand Chat, Baie du lièvre, Baie au lapin tell of the boredom of a long sailing trip where the tiniest incident, a hare escaping, the ship's cat sleeping on a coil of rope at the moment land is sighted, everything becomes an event.

Album Rock, according to Thoulet, is "a reminder of an episode that involved Admiral Cloué … The admiral had collected a number of picturesque views of the country and had the idea, for the title page of his album, to have the word *Album* written in huge letters on this cliff and to photograph it."

Thoulet's visit to Sacred Bay must have been much different than mine, and I can't help but be amused by his uncharacteristically snarky remarks:

> *Sacred Bay is not very beautiful to look at; it is a wide expanse of water without character, bordered by hills of medium height, covered with endless dwarf fir trees. Mosquitos and blackflies seem to have chosen it as their headquarters; seldom have they been worse than this: every boat that comes ashore is followed during the return trip out by a cloud of the insects, which fiercely and unrelentingly attack the faces of the sailors, who cannot take their hands from the oars to drive them off. . . .*

> *The interior of the bay is dotted with isolated rocks, one of which is named the Mauvais Gars [Bad Lad] Rock. What vessel must have encountered problems there, that its crew, unable to do anything better or worse, took revenge by giving it this insulting name?*

Terre Neuve l'été, complètement inabordable à cause de sa garnison ailée (Newfoundland in the summer, completely inaccessible because of its winged garrison), Louis Koenig.

Pierre Neuve l'été, complètement
ordable à cause de sa garnison ailée.

Where is Miot in 1886, while Thoulet is rephotographing his rock? Possibly in Madagascar, or possibly on the other side of the camera, having his photo taken by Nadar, the "mauvais gars" of Parisian photography. Nadar would have appreciated Miot's inventive use of his camera for hydrographic work—he famously took to a hot-air balloon to make the world's first aerial photographs, and descended into Parisian catacombs to make the first photographs using artificial light.

I found four Atelier Nadar portraits of Miot in the archives of the Bibliothèque Nationale, three depicting Miot as a middle-aged *Capitaine* and one as an elderly *Vice Amiral*. It's easy to imagine Miot and Nadar striking up a friendship over the years, discussing innovations in photographic technology, or the difficulties of balancing a camera on a swaying balloon or ship.

Curiously, the Bibliothèque database lists the date for all four Nadar portraits as 1900, the year of Miot's death, even though Miot has aged about 20 years in the final image. Looking at Thoulet's photo again, it's fascinating to see how both Album Rock and Miot have transfigured over the decades—like the rock, Miot has fewer tufts of vegetation on his head. But in all of the Nadar photos he sports the same imposing mutton chops and gentle jawline, and has the same eyes.

Capitaine Miot, Atelier Nadar (BnF).

In the series of younger portraits especially, Miot's eyes have a stern, wearied kindness. From the numbers on the photos, we can see that he begins the photographic session sitting, then stands and leans on a pedestal. At first the corner of his mouth holds the hint of a smile, as if he finds the whole rigamarole amusing, but by the third image it languishes into a kind of grimace. The backdrop is blank, as unforthcoming as the skies in Miot's Newfoundland landscapes. And the sequence of three portraits is eerily reminiscent of his own three photographs of the Mi'kmaq woman on the deck of the *Sésostris*, visibly aggravated as she exposes her breast.

Among Paul-Émile Miot's fellow chroniclers of 19th-century oceans is Herman Melville, who likewise spent years as a sailor in the Pacific. Melville fictionalized his experiences in Tahiti and the Marquesas Islands in novels such as *Typee: A Peep at Polynesian Life*, though he's of course best known for writing *Moby-Dick*. Noting many similarities in Miot's and Melville's interpretations of Tahiti, art historian Sydney Picasso suggests in her book *The Invention of Paradise* that their works helped popularize the Western fantasy of a carefree island utopia.

Picasso praises Miot's "perfect balance of passion and observation." In the same way that Melville's novels fuse experience and imagination, she argues, Miot's landscapes bridge the territories of documentary and art. "The photographer has inserted figures in the photo, and this apparition is another 'proof' of human presence," she writes. "The factual quality in the photos is underlined in this manner, but it is also the seed of a narrative, as in 'I was here'—a more expressive form of graffiti. Herman Melville in the same way uses seeds of observation in his texts so that the reader is impressed by the 'fact,' while being serenaded by the 'poetry.'"

Miot's photos of the French Shore are quite literally meant to say "we are here" (or, when he documents British intrusion into French territory: "you are here, and you're not supposed to be!"). *Album Rock* says something more. It's easy to fall under its spell, to be seduced by its poetry. I keep wanting to turn it into a story. But like Miot's Mi'kmaq portraits, it records more than how just one individual

understood the world. It can also be seen to demonstrate how European colonizers used both image and language to assert dominance over other cultures.

"All over the world during the nineteenth century," writes John Berger in *Another Way of Telling*, "European travellers, soldiers, colonial administrators, adventurers, took photographs of 'the natives,' their customs, their architecture, their richness, their poverty, their women's breasts, their headdresses; and these images, besides provoking amazement, were presented and read as proof of the justice of the imperial division of the world. The division between those who organised and rationalised and surveyed, and those who *were* surveyed."

"Landscape," cultural theorist W.J.T. Mitchell declares, "doesn't merely signify or symbolize power relations; it is an instrument of cultural power." Miot's photos are not merely postcards, but can be understood as land claims. His Newfoundland landscapes were used to assert ownership of the French Shore, while his scenes of Tahitian life enticed opportunists such as Paul Gauguin, who went to Polynesia not just to paint but to marry 13-year-old indigenous girls. Miot's photos of Mi'kmaq women were used to reinforce Gobineau's sickening stereotypes.

Album, in Latin, means literally "whiteness"; it is the noun form of *albus*, the colour white. Miot's prints are *albumen prints* because egg whites were used to bind the photographic chemicals to the paper. Having sailors paint the word *Album* might have been a whimsical act, a way to pass an afternoon. Still, I can't help but also read the image as a sort of unwitting paean to colonialism. By inscribing *whiteness* on the landscape, a whiteness that lingers 160 years later, *Album Rock* exemplifies the power of naming, of written language as a means of asserting ownership. Miot is a naval officer, an artist, and, we should remember, an agent of exploitation and conquest.

"It was the whiteness of the whale that above all things appalled me," as Ishmael puts it in *Moby-Dick*. Like Melville's ghostly whale, Miot can be both fascinating and appalling. He's also extremely elusive, and it would take a lifetime to trace his escapades beyond Newfoundland and across the world's oceans to Mexico, Uruguay, Tahiti, Tunisia, and Madagascar. Having chased him for as long as I can, I'm content to lie on the moss on this oddly shaped rock in Sacred Bay and catch my breath.

Belying its black and white surface, *Album Rock* is iridescent. It shimmers with questions and contradictions, beckons us in. Miot, after all, intended to use it as the cover of a collection of photos. It's meant as an invitation.

La baie des îles ou le rendez-vous des aquilons (Bay of islands or the north winds meet), Louis Koenig.

TIMELINE—MIOT IN NEWFOUNDLAND

1827–1843

February 11, 1827: Paul-Émile Miot is born in Trinidad. His grandfather had come to Santo Domingo from Bordeaux, and Miot's father moved to Trinidad and married Rose-Henriette Mongenot, who was from Martinique, in 1824. Miot is sent to boarding school in Ireland, where he learns English.

1843–1849

November 5, 1843: Miot attends the École Navale in France, receiving the rank of ensign. In 1848, a report card describes him as "[i]ncapable, lazy, and having relations with his subordinates based on addressing them with threats and calling them most improper names."

1851–1853

Miot travels to the West Indies aboard the *Sibyl* and *Cérès*. He was named *Chevalier de la Légion d'honneur* for taking charge of the *Cérès* after its crew was decimated by yellow fever. A photo of the *Cérès* in dry dock in Dieppe taken around this time (Library and Archives Canada dates it 1854–1855) is possibly one of Miot's earliest photographs.

1854–1855

May 9–July 10: Miot voyages to the Baltic Sea aboard the *Asmodée*.

1855–1856

October 24–March 30: During the Crimean War, Miot serves aboard the *Uranie* and the *Laplace*. He most likely meets Georges-Charles Cloué (1817–1889) during this period. Cloué, who soon becomes Miot's captain and collaborator, had already worked as a hydrographer in Newfoundland in 1849, 1850–1851, and 1852–1853.

1857: FIRST VOYAGE TO NEWFOUNDLAND

February 28: Miot boards the *Ardent*, a small steam-powered vessel commanded by Captain Cloué. They leave for Newfoundland on March 27, and Miot brings his collodion photography equipment.

July 30: Miot is appointed lieutenant.

September 27: In St. John's, Cloué writes a letter to Louis Mazères, commodore of the Newfoundland station, in which he praises Miot's hydrographic work and explains the process. "Mr. Miot's camera has a lens of 0m085 and has only plates measuring 0m27 by 0m22 with which one can record only a field of view of approximately 25 degrees … with five views from a powerful instrument, one could obtain most of the necessary readings. Three carefully-selected camera locations within a broad area would be sufficient to obtain a reproduction of the land and the indentations of the coast with the greatest accuracy."

November 10: The ship returns to Paris.

1858: SECOND VOYAGE TO NEWFOUNDLAND

February 12: A month before his second trip to Newfoundland, Miot becomes a member of the Société française de photographie, which was founded in 1854.

March 13–November 11: Miot embarks on a hydrographic mission to Newfoundland aboard the *Sésostris*. In 1858 the Naval Division of Newfoundland was captained by Camille Clément, Baron de La Roncière Le Noury (1813–1881). La Roncière wrote many letters home to his wife and daughter, and reports of June 15: "On coming back we stopped at a small island where we took some sea gull's eggs and also seven little gulls recently hatched, which I am trying to raise."

1859: THIRD VOYAGE TO NEWFOUNDLAND

March 13–November 5: Another hydrographic mission to Newfoundland aboard the *Sésostris*. During this trip, Miot likely meets Count Joseph Arthur de Gobineau (1816–1882), a French diplomat and member of the Anglo-French Commission, who visited the French Shore from June 15 to August 27. Gobineau describes spending a few hours on the *Sésostris* on June 28, when the Commission met there.

Also in 1859, several of Miot's photos of the fishery in Newfoundland and St-Pierre and Miquelon are used as references by Louis Le Breton (1818–1866), draftsman at the Maps and Plans Department in Paris. Le Breton's engravings accompany an article by the pseudonymous N. O'Brig published in *L'Illustration, journal universel*.

1860: FOURTH VOYAGE TO NEWFOUNDLAND

March 22—November 18: Miot again leaves on a hydrographic mission to Newfoundland aboard the *Sésostris*. On July 24, the *Sésostris* is in St. John's during a ceremony to mark the official landing of Albert Edward (Edward VII), Prince of Wales, who was touring North America.

1861–1862: FIFTH VOYAGE TO NEWFOUNDLAND

April 4–October 18: Miot's final hydrographic mission to Newfoundland aboard the *Milan*. Over his five journeys, it's believed that Miot made about 80 photographs of the island.

1862

Miot officially establishes the first photographic atelier at the Dépôt des Cartes et Plans de la Marine (it had gotten started on his initiative in 1857).

Capitaine Georges-Charles Cloué à bord du navire l'Ardent (Captain Georges-Charles Cloué on board the Ardent), Paul-Émile Miot.

1863

July 21: Miot leaves Paris to command the *Adonis* during the Second French Intervention in Mexico.

Also in 1863, Gobineau's "Voyage à Terre-Neuve" (first published in 1861) is reprinted in *Le Tour du Monde*, with engravings that are clearly based on Miot's Newfoundland photos, including his Mi'kmaq portraits.

1863–1867

Miot takes part in naval missions in Mexico and Martinique.

1868

Cloué finishes writing his *Pilote de Terre Neuve*, a navigational guide to the coast of Newfoundland.

July 17: Miot boards the *Astrée* as chief of the Pacific division commanded by Cloué.

1868–1871

Aboard the frigate *Astrée*, Miot travels in 1868 to Montevideo (Uruguay), in 1869 to San Francisco (USA), Valparaíso (Chile) and Papeete (Tahiti), then in 1870 again to Chile and the Marquesas Islands.

The 1870 odyssey of the *Astrée* is described by Louise Berenger in *Le Fret maritime dans les Îles Pacifique Sud*: "After stops in the Canary Islands, in Saint Vincent of Cape Verde, in Montevideo, she passed through the Magellan Canal and the side canals of Patagonia, where she damaged the keel and bow on a rock. Then there are stops on the shores of South America. In Callao, Peru, the damage was repaired. Then Panama, San Francisco … Fort Alcatraz and its giant guns. It then stops at Esquimalt Bay (Vancouver Island, British Columbia), then San Francisco again, and finally Papeete."

From June 22 to September 1, 1870, the *Astrée* is in Papeete. Biographer Yves Leroy reports that on the *Astrée* Miot "had installed a real shooting studio," and Miot's photos of Tahiti and the Marquesas Islands are perhaps his best-known work. They include many portraits of indigenous islanders that are reminiscent of his Mi'kmaq photographs, including the Queen of Tahiti, Pōmare IV, who visits the *Astrée* on August 15, 1870.

On January 14, 1871, having taken ill, Miot is repatriated to France. The *Astrée* continues to Senegal, where Félix Auguste Le Clerc (1838–1896), a fellow naval officer, continues the documentary work, probably with Miot's equipment. It's likely that Miot was Le Clerc's photographic mentor. Le Clerc married Cloué's daughter in October 1867, and in April 1871 he was placed in charge of the photography department at the Dépôt des Cartes et Plans de la Marine (which had been started by Miot).

1873–1888

Miot's military career continues. He commands many ships and travels widely, participating in campaigns in Tunisia (where, following the occupation of Bizerte, he is made governor for a few weeks) and Madagascar. He is promoted to captain, rear admiral, and finally vice admiral.

In 1885 and 1886, Félix Auguste Le Clerc commands the *Clorinde* on voyages to Newfoundland. In 1885 Louis Koenig (1847–1920) makes a series of wonderful watercolours documenting the trip, as well as a cartoon journal that he gives to Le Clerc as a gift. On the 1886 voyage (which Koenig also took part in), Julien Thoulet (1843–1936) rephotographs Album Rock.

1889
December 25: Georges-Charles Cloué dies.

1892
February: Miot leaves active service.

1894
May: Miot is appointed curator of the Musée de la Marine at the Louvre. In 1898 he authors a booklet titled *Promenades au musée de la marine,* which describes the rooms and collections of the museum.

1900
December 6: Miot, who never married, dies in Paris.

IMAGE CREDITS

Cover and pages 0, 24, 33, 85: Paul-Émile Miot, *Rocher peint par les marins français* (1857-1859). Library and Archives Canada / PA-188210

Pages 3, 8, 18, 23, 25, 26, 30, 34, 41, 42, 49, 56, 63: Photos by Matthew Hollett.

Page 5: *Le Pilote de Terre-Neuve* (1784). Memorial University of Newfoundland Digital Archives Initiative. http://collections.mun.ca/cdm/ref/collection/maps/id/203

Page 7: *Chart of the island of Newfoundland* (1801), Memorial University of Newfoundland Digital Archives Initiative. http://collections.mun.ca/cdm/ref/collection/maps/id/240

Page 11: Paul-Émile Miot, *St. John's taken from Signal Hill* (1857-1859). Library and Archives Canada / PA-195496

Page 13: Photo by Adam Durocher.

Page 15: Paul-Émile Miot, *Vue du Capitaine Georges-Charles Cloué sur le pont du navire l'Ardent* (1857). Library and Archives Canada / PA-194617

Page 16: Louis Koenig, *Près de l'île Kirpon (Near Kirpon Island)* (1885). Library and Archives Canada / R11617-31-5-F

Page 20: Paul-Émile Miot, *Fabrication de l'huile de morue à Terre-Neuve*. Library and Archives Canada / PA-194629

Page 29: Paul-Émile Miot, *Sur le pont du navire l'Ardent avant son départ* (1857). Library and Archives Canada / PA-194623

Page 36: Louis Koenig, *Retour du beau temps (The return of pleasant weather)* (1885). Library and Archives Canada / R11617-17-0-F

Pages 38, 67: Paul-Émile Miot, *Marins français dans les rochers (Nord de Terre-Neuve)* (1857-1859). Library and Archives Canada / PA-188211

Pages 44, 55, 64: Paul-Émile Miot, *Rocher peint par les marins français* (1857-1859), rephotographed by Matthew Hollett.

Page 47: Louis Koenig, *Aspect de glaces, près du Kirpon (Views of ice, near Kirpon)* (1885). Library and Archives Canada / R12330-25-8-F

Page 51: Paul-Émile Miot, *Portrait d'un marin pris à bord du navire l'Ardent* (1857). Library and Archives Canada / PA-194620

Page 52: Paul-Émile Miot, *Avisos à roues au mouillage (Nord de Terre-Neuve)* (1857-1859). Library and Archives Canada / PA-188224

Page 58: Paul-Émile Miot, *Femme Mi'kmaq à bord du navire Sésostris* (near Sydney, Nova Scotia, 1859). Library and Archives Canada / PA-188213

Page 61: Jerry Evans, *We Were Not the Savages* (lithograph, 1998).

Page 69: Georges-Charles Cloué, *Plan de la Baie du Sacre (Côte Nord de Terre-Neuve)* (1857), rephotographed by Matthew Hollett.

Pages 70, 71: Georges-Charles Cloué, *Pilote de Terre Neuve* (1869), rephotographed by Matthew Hollett.

Page 72: Louis Koenig, *À bord de l'Ibis en tournée sur la côte Est (On board the Ibis touring the east coast)* (1885). Library and Archives Canada / R11617-40-6-F

Page 75: Julien Thoulet. *Vue 28*, from *42 phot. de Saint-Pierre et Miquelon, de Cap-Breton, de Terre-Neuve, du Labrador* (1887). Bibliothèque nationale de France. http://gallica.bnf.fr/ark:/12148/btv1b6700402k/

Page 78: Paul-Émile Miot, *Aviso français l'Ardent accosté à une estacade de bois* (1857). Library and Archives Canada / PA-188217

Page 81: Louis Koenig, *Terre Neuve l'été, complètement inabordable à cause de sa garnison ailée (Newfoundland in the summer, completely inaccessible because of its winged garrison)* (1885). Library and Archives Canada / R11617-25-X-F

Page 83: Atelier Nadar. *Capitaine Miot.* Bibliothèque nationale de France. http://gallica.bnf.fr/ark:/12148/btv1b53104376k/

Page 88: Louis Koenig, *La baie des îles ou le rendez-vous des aquilons (Bay of islands or the north winds meet)* (1885). Library and Archives Canada / R11617-30-3-F

Page 93: Paul-Émile Miot, *Capitaine Georges-Charles Cloué à bord du navire l'Ardent* (1857). Library and Archives Canada / PA-194627

Page 100: Louis Koenig, *Au mouillage de la Baie du Sacre* (1885). Library and Archives Canada / R12330-33-7-F

Page 104: Félix Auguste Le Clerc, *Prenant un Ris à Bord de L'Astrée* (1871), Metropolitan Museum of Art. https://www.metmuseum.org/art/collection/search/306173

Page 107: Paul-Émile Miot, *Cod preparation* (1857-1859). Library and Archives Canada / PA-202293

Au mouillage de la Baie du Sacre *au petit hàvre* Mercredi 9 Sept. 85. – Au mouillage de la baie Du Sacre –. *Vue prise du bord de la Clorinde Île du Mouillé*

Au mouillage de la Baie du Sacre (Anchorage at Sacred Bay), Louis Koenig.

Phare et cap Boult

la rade de l'ouest.   cap d'Artimon

REFERENCES

Berenger, Louise. *Le Fret maritime dans les Îles Pacifique Sud.* 2008. http://memsic.ccsd.cnrs.fr/mem_00000655/document.

Cellem, Robert. *Visit of His Royal Highness the Prince of Wales to the British North American Provinces and United States in the Year 1860.* Toronto: Henry Rowsell, 1861. http://collections.mun.ca/cdm/compoundobject/collection/cns2/id/25830/rec/1.

Chomette, Michèle, and Pierre Mard Richard. *Paul-Émile Miot (1827–1900), un marin photographe.* Paris: Éditions Galerie Michèle Chomette, 1995.

Cloué, Georges-Charles. *Pilote de Terre Neuve.* Paris: Typographie Adolphe Laine, 1869.

Cloué, Georges-Charles. "Carte Particulière de la Côte Nord de Terre-Neuve comprise entre Le Cap d'Oignon et les Iles Blanches." The Rooms Archives, French Hydrographic Charts collection, No. 1453 (1854).

Cloué, Georges-Charles. "Plan de la Baie du Sacre (Côte Nord de Terre-Neuve)." The Rooms Archives, French Hydrographic Charts collection, No. 1704 (1857).

De Gobineau, Joseph Arthur. *A Gentleman in the Outports: Gobineau and Newfoundland.* Edited and translated by Michael Wilkshire. Ottawa: Carleton University Press, 1993.

"Francophones of Newfoundland & Labrador." Corner Brook Museum & Archives. http://www.virtualmuseum.ca/sgc-cms/histoires_de_chez_nous-community_memories/pm_v2.php?id=exhibit_home&fl=0&lg=English&ex=00000301.

"Georges-Charles Cloué." École Navale. http://ecole.nav.traditions.free.fr/officiers_cloue_georges.htm.

Gobineau, J.A. "Voyage à Terre-Neuve." *Le Tour du Monde* 1er semestre (1863): 401–16. http://gallica.bnf.fr/ark:/12148/bpt6k34382j/f404.image.

Jamieson, Scott, and Anne Thareau, ed. and trans. *French Visitors to Newfoundland*. St. John's: ISER Books, 2013.

"Jerry Evans." Updated July 2013. http://www.heritage.nf.ca/articles/arts/jerry-evans.php.

Leroy, Yves. "Paul-Émile Miot." *Annales du Patrimoine de Fécamp* 10 (2003). http://www.lucien-girardin.com/histoire4c.html.

Melville, Herman. *Moby-Dick: Or, the Whale*. New York: Penguin Books, 2001.
Mitchell, W.J.T. *Landscape and Power*. 2nd ed. Chicago & London: University of Chicago Press, 2002.

Morris, Errol. *Believing Is Seeing: Observations on the Mysteries of Photography*. New York: Penguin, 2011.

Nadar, Felix. *When I Was a Photographer*. Translated by Eduardo Cadava and Liana Theodoratou. Cambridge: MIT Press, 2015.

"Paul-Émile Miot." École Navale. http://ecole.nav.traditions.free.fr/officiers_miot.htm.

O'Brig, N. "Terre-Neuve." Pts. 1 and 2. *L'Illustration, journal universel* (March 19, 1859): 183–86; (April 2, 1859): 215–18.

Picasso, Sydney. *The Invention of Paradise: Photographs by Paul-Émile Miot*. Munich: Galerie Daniel Blau, 2008.

Rompkey, Ronald. "The Representation of Newfoundland in Nineteenth-Century French Travel Literature." *Newfoundland and Labrador Studies* 25, no. 2 (2010). https://journals.lib.unb.ca/index.php/nflds/article/view/18352/19796.

Sontag, Susan. *Regarding the Pain of Others*. London: Penguin Books, 2003.

Thoulet, Julian. *A Voyage to Newfoundland*. Translated by Scott Jamieson. Montreal & Kingston: McGill-Queen's University Press, 2005.

Tompkins, Edward. *Ktaqmkukewaq Mi'kmaq: Wlqatmuti / The Mi'kmaw People of Newfoundland: A Celebration*. Corner Brook: Federation of Newfoundland Indians, 2004.

White, Mary M. "Vice-Admiral Clément de La Roncière in Newfoundland Waters in 1858." *Newfoundland Quarterly* 75, no. 3 (1979): 35–44.

Wilkshire, Michael, and Gerald Penney. "Five Micmac Photographs." *Newfoundland Quarterly* 86, no. 3 (1991): 12–16.

Wilkshire, Michael, and Gerald Penney. "Paul-Émile Miot: 19th Century Photographer of Newfoundland." *Newfoundland Quarterly* 88, no. 4 (1994): 3–4.

Wilkshire, Michael, and Gerald Penney. "Paul-Émile Miot in Newfoundland." November 2012. http://www.ucs.mun.ca/~mwilks/miot.html.

Prenant un Ris à Bord de l'Astrée (Taking a Risk on the Astrée), Félix Auguste Le Clerc, 1871.

ACKNOWLEDGMENTS

This book would not exist without the expertise and imagination of many wonderful people. Michael Wilkshire (Memorial University, retired) and Lori Pauli (Curator of Photography at the National Gallery of Canada) were endlessly helpful, and pointed me in many right directions. Thanks also to Jerry Evans, Samantha Shields at Library and Archives Canada, the staff at The Rooms Archives, Joan Simmonds at the French Shore Historical Society, and George French at the Corner Brook Museum & Archives.

My immense thanks to everyone at Boulder Publications, especially Gavin and Amanda Will for believing in this project, Stephanie Porter for her editing finesse, and Todd Manning for his fantastic book design.

Thanks to Rosie Myers for the road trip! I would never have made it to Ship Cove on foot.

Finally, I gratefully acknowledge the support of ArtsNL through their Professional Project Grant program.

Cod preparation, Paul-Émile Miot.

ABOUT THE AUTHOR

Matthew Hollett is a writer and visual artist in St. John's, Newfoundland and Labrador. His poetry manuscript, *Optic Nerve*, won the 2017 NLCU Fresh Fish Award for Emerging Writers. Matthew was awarded the 2018 Cox & Palmer SPARKS Creative Writing Award, *The Fiddlehead*'s 2018 Ralph Gustafson Prize for Best Poem, and the *Malahat Review*'s 2017 Open Season Award for Creative Nonfiction.